A Voice from Elsewhere

SUNY series, Insinuations:
Philosophy, Psychoanalysis, Literature

Charles Shepherdson, editor

A Voice from Elsewhere

Maurice Blanchot

Translated by
Charlotte Mandell

STATE UNIVERSITY OF NEW YORK PRESS

Published in French as *Une voix venue d'ailleurs* © Editions Gallimard, Paris, 2002.

Published by
State University of New York Press, Albany

Ouvrage publié avec le concours du Ministère français chargé de la culture—Centre national du livre

This book was published with the assistance of the French Ministry of Culture / National Book Center

For information, address State University of New York Press, 194 Washington Avenue, Suite 305, Albany, NY 12210-2384

Production by Diane Ganeles
Marketing by Anne M. Valentine

Library of Congress Cataloging-in-Publication Data

Blanchot, Maurice.
    [Voix venue d'ailleurs. English]
    A voice from elsewhere / Maurice Blanchot ; translated by Charlotte Mandell.
        p. cm. — (Suny series, insinuations—philosophy, psychoanalysis, literature)
    Includes bibliographical references and index.
    ISBN-13: 978-0-7914-7015-2 (hardcover : alk. paper)
    ISBN-13: 978-0-7914-7016-9 (pbk. : alk. paper)
    I. Mandell, Charlotte. II. Title.

PQ2603.L3343V6513 2007
843'.912—dc22   2006032534

10 9 8 7 6 5 4 3 2 1

Contents

Translator's Note

I would like to thank Monique Antelme, lifelong friend of Maurice Blanchot, for her kind words of encouragement. I would also like to thank Christophe Bident for his ever-helpful biography of Blanchot, *Maurice Blanchot: Partenaire invisible*.

I am very grateful to Charles Shepherdson, editor of this series, both for his informed enthusiasm for Blanchot's work, and for including this text in the series. I thank James Peltz, director of SUNY Press, for his help.

I am deeply indebted to Leslie Hill for sending me a copy of the 1986 Fata Morgana *édition définitive* of *Le dernier à parler* (which I used as reference for the present translation) along with a copy of the earlier version of the same text that appeared in the 1972 *Revue des belles lettres*, and for his help in locating the original Celan texts.

I am grateful to Michael Naas for his thorough reading of this text in manuscript; his comments and suggestions were invaluable.

I am also grateful to Éric Trudel for his thorough reading of my translation of *Anacrouse*, and for his generous commentary on the poems of Louis-René des Forêts, whose work he has studied and enjoyed.

My husband, the poet Robert Kelly, was especially helpful in the Celan and Char chapters, and his careful reading and thoughtful revisions of the entire book were deeply appreciated.

I would also like to thank Kevin Hart, Marina van Zuylen, and Odile Chilton for their much-needed support and advice.

A note about the Celan chapter: my translations of the Celan poems are only from Blanchot's own French translations of the original texts—not from the German. Blanchot's readings of the German into French are often quite free, both in meaning and in arrangement of the text.

Several texts in this book have been translated before: Leslie Hill's "The Beast of Lascaux" appeared in the *Oxford Literary Review*, No. 22, 2000, pp. 9–18; "The Last One to Speak," as translated by

Joseph Simas, appeared in *Translating Tradition: Paul Celan in France*, a special double issue (#8/9) of ACTS: A Journal of New Writing, 1988, pp. 228–239; "Michel Foucault as I Imagine Him," as translated by Jeffrey Mehlman, was published in *Foucault/Blanchot*, New York: Zone Books, 1990, pp. 61–109. *Ostinato*, by Louis-René des Forêts, has been translated by Mary Ann Caws for University of Nebraska Press, 2002. I used all these translations as reference; my only reason for translating them anew is my firm belief that there can never be enough translations of a given text, especially one as subtle and full of nuance as a text by Blanchot. Just as every new book brings us a little closer to the Mallarméan concept of the Ideal Book, so every translation brings us closer (we hope) to the original. Fortunately although the Ideal Translation may not exist, the Ideal Reader—you, reading this—does, and he or she likely has blue pencil in hand.

CHARLOTTE MANDELL

Anacrusis

On the Poems
of Louis-René des Forêts

May the child's voice in him never be silenced, may it fall like a gift from the sky offering to dried-out words the brilliance of his laughter, the salt of his tears, his all-powerful savagery.

—Louis-René des Forêts
from *Ostinato*

A Voice from Elsewhere

When I was living in Èze, in the little room (made bigger by two views, one opening onto Corsica, the other out past Cap Ferrat) where I most often stayed, there was (there still is), hanging on the wall, the likeness of the girl they called "The Unknown Girl from the Seine," an adolescent with closed eyes, but alive with such a fine, blissful (but veiled) smile, that one might have thought she had drowned in an instant of extreme happiness. So unlike his own works, she had seduced Giacometti to such a point that he looked for a young woman who might have been willing to undergo anew the test of that felicity in death.

Anacrouse initially appeared under the title "Une voix venue d'ailleurs," from Éditions Ulysse, in 1992.

The poems by Louis-René des Forêts to which Maurice Blanchot's texts refer are collected in *Les Mégères de la mer* (Mercure de France) and *Poèmes de Samuel Wood* (Fata Morgana). "The White / The Black" refers to extracts from *Ostinato* (Mercure de France; English edition: University of Nebraska Press, translated by Mary Ann Caws, 2002).

5

It is out of tact that I evoke this image, in order not to alter the haunting quality of the poems of Samuel Wood—Samuel la Forêt—where there rises up in the night dream the childlike figure, sometimes smiling among the asters and roses, standing "in the full light of her grace" or holding up a candle that she blows out as if reluctantly so that she won't be seen disappearing. "*She makes herself seen only in dreams / Too beautiful to put the suffering to sleep*" and on the contrary aggravating it since she is there only in dreams, a presence about which we know at the same time that it is deceiving. Deceiving?

"*No, she is there, really there / What does it matter if sleep takes advantage of us.*"

It would be better to abandon prudent reason and destroy the daytime wisdom that seeks to destroy "*the wonderful apparition / Welcomed as one trembles at the sight of a face seized by death.*" "*She is there to watch over us / Who go to sleep only to see her.*"

Thus the dream and the rational day pursue an unceasing battle.

"*A dream, but is there anything more real than a dream?*" And how can one survive without dreaming "*That the child, drawn to her familiar places / Comes into this garden of roses, and every night / Returns to fill the*

6

bedroom with her candid flame / That she holds out to us like an offering and a prayer"?

"*There is also that woman seated on a window ledge / And she is always the same. Who is she, then? What sign is she making with her fingers gloved in red?*" And if we tear ourselves from sleep to question her and lose her, here she is again, returning on the following nights in a similar posture, resting against another window.

A figure that disturbs me, since I have met her too, but during the day, diurnal and spectral. Messenger of Melancholy, so similar to the apparition evoked by Henry James in *The Turn of the Screw*, motionless like a woman conscious of her guilt, slightly turned away so that we can escape from the memory of our own guilt.

Figures that are too real to last.

And that is when the questioning that exposes the illusion intervenes: "*These visions were only an error of oblivion.*" It is forbidden "to ignore the laws of nature" and pretend to checkmate death. Samuel Wood or his double utters the judgment: "*Irreparable crack. Let us take note of it. / Now we are sorry as long as we live.*"

But then another temptation occurs: why not cut the moorings so as to go toward her in death, by

7

a death that is not only consented to, but summoned, *"chosen like the perfect form of silence"*?

Or, in another realistic perspective, why not wait for the memory to weaken, ceasing *"to suffer by ceasing to see her / Joining us on nights favorable to encounters"*?

A temptation that rejects "the uncompromising boy," the one we learned to know before in "Une mémoire démentielle" [A demented memory], who formulates the implacable sentence.

"To unite with nothingness, nothing engenders nothing."

And there again is the effort of a rigor for which forgetting even what we call oblivion brings no consolation, all the while sustaining another survival, an infinitely more obscure demand: *"The tenderness that keeps the voice throttled / The duty of vigilant friendship."*

"The duty of vigilant friendship." What agitation we feel at these words that are so simple, so beautiful. Whatever the objections may be, the oscillations by which *"attraction and terror go hand in hand,"* we are no longer permitted to be silent. You must speak (even if speaking has always had either too much or too little meaning). Scarcely have you made this resolution, than the "you must be quiet" comes back: it is better "*to abandon the leaves in progress that clutter up your table.*" "*Silence itself tells more about it than words. And everything that speaks is made of mortal flesh.*" But let us speak, for we have no other instruments but words, which "*remain our masters in all things / Since we have to make use of them in order to be quiet.*"

This is when the dreamer interrogates the figure who lends him a byname and thus unburdens him of it. "*You about whom nothing says that you live under this name, Samuel, Samuel, is it really your voice I hear / Coming as if from the depths of a tomb / To strengthen my own voice struggling with words / Or to act as echo to its great destitution?*"

The answer is within each one of us and we know that, close to death, we still have to "*keep watch in silence,*" to welcome the secret friendship by which some voice from elsewhere comes to make itself heard. Vain voice? Perhaps.

It matters little. What has SPOKEN to us will always speak to us, just as we never stop hearing (is it eternity?) the final harmony extinguished in [Messiaen's] "Quartet for the End of Time."

9

Rough Draft of a Regret

I wrote this commentary (or what seems to pass as a commentary), and while I was writing it, led along by the movement that is the gift of the poem, I closed my eyes to my fault, which lies in transforming the poem (the poems) into a prose approximation. There is no alteration graver than that. These poems by Samuel Wood have their voice, which one must hear before thinking one understands them. *On a touché au vers* ["The line has been meddled with"—a phrase of Mallarmé's]. But Mallarmé still recognized in "free verse" the old "worn-out" alexandrine. How I would like to be able to express the rhythm that, prolonging the ancient line, gives it a somber, sometimes solar glory—the sublime within simplicity—yet here, by these epithets, I stifle the voices that summon us and draw us toward the ultimate point.

The White   The Black

I think we have to speak of *Ostinato*, but we would have to speak of it without words, in a language that haunts me by failing me.

Ostinato is a musical notation. It is a theme without variations, a stubborn motif that returns and doesn't return. Alban Berg hears it in Schumann, and I too hear it as that single note that kept resounding in his head without being able to develop.

It is also "the obstinate rigor" of Leonardo da Vinci whose enchantment the young Paul Valéry experienced, while committing himself to retain only its rigor.

However, with Louis-René des Forêts, we come up against a central difficulty. I suppose an immense, infinite, irremediable catastrophe occurred in his life. The abyss, absolute disaster. After which he was deprived of the gifts of writing. I do not think there was an oath: "I will not write anymore." An oath that did not need to be uttered. Shipwreck in which the one who wrote was as if swallowed up. "*See here, in the corner in the very bottom of the virgin canvas, the remnants of a shipwreck.*"

I dare say that that it was real (alas). For years, the writer stopped writing. And, as if to make such an interruption even more fatal, he spent his time in other arts: painting, drawing—music, perhaps, for all I know.

How was he one day brought back to the demand of writing, which neither suffering, nor the unspoken vow, nor perpetual emptiness succeeded in conquering? Perhaps he realized that, in order to stop writing, one has to continue to write, to write end-lessly until the end, or starting from the end.

There are no white spaces unless there is black, no silence unless speech and noise are produced, in order to cease.

Thence (but that is not the only reason) the fragmentary disposition, the discontinuity of the text of *Ostinato*. I know from experience that nothing is more perilous than writing that lacks narrative sequence or the necessary movement of argumentation. If one follows a trajectory, it is "*a blind trajectory.*" One goes nowhere. The commodity of a goal, even a distant one, does not exist. Nor do maxims, or aphorisms, or expressive words, and even less the anything-goes of automatic writing.

Are we dealing with an autobiography? That would be to misjudge the text, written in the present (outside *durée*) and calling into question someone always designated in the third person, without being able to recognize in it a distant "I," already neutral, even impersonal. (The previous récits by Louis-René des Forêts were most often written in the first person, and already had a particular status, I without I, a mode in which questioning, uncertainty were at play, the balance between the real and the imaginary.)

The present in *Ostinato* has various characteristics: sometimes hidden recollections that an incomparable memory—a tragic memory—brings back to light, compels to experience again as if it hadn't already happened, as if to experience its actuality once again; sometimes an epiphanic message that has a sovereign beauty, even if implacable awareness seeks afterward to betray its glamour—sometimes . . . but I'll interrupt myself: it is up to each reader to pursue, to sound out, its riches.

I'll return to the obligation of speaking, of writing, which the author experienced, after a long silence, as a condemnation, even a damnation. "*To be silent, no, he no longer had the means, even if he knew a trembling of hatred and fear in hearing his voice climb back up from the abyss where he thought he had forever cast and lost it. No, he no longer had any strength to resist it, unconscious, veiled perhaps, but still there, insistent, unwavering, as if to catch him while his vigilance lapsed, and throw him back into a new torment.*"

That is why, in my turn, I will be silent, incapable of bearing the insufficiency of commentary and of reestablishing the main thread connecting the elements of a discourse that tries to make us hear the *ultima verba*, the haunting fear of definitive fracture.

O Ostinato, o bitter beauty.

Anacrusis

I will content myself (already an unacceptable word, since it suggests contentment) with trying to understand the Lyotard text called "The Survivor,"[1] while continuing to meditate on the poems published under the signature Louis-René des Forêts.

Where is the beginning? Is it someone, or something, that is beginning?

We have Hegel's answer: death is the life of the spirit. "The spirit does not survive death; it is the sublation [la relève] of immediate life ... Spirit lives only insofar as it is dead to what it itself WAS ... Its previous form is no longer living." The result of this, and it is very important: "The entity I was can no longer say 'I.'" "I" can no longer speak for itself THEN except in the third person. That is how Hegel comes to "we" (we, that is to say, I then and I now). Thus nothing is lost. Death is always a good death, since it is "retained" in the "we" that the me-then and the me-now form together.

But is nothing really lost? What is necessarily lost is the "alive" presence THEN of what is NOW. The contingency is lost, and we can question the presence of "then." And time itself, which is reduced to being only the sublation of one mode by another, is lost. Of course, the flight of the owl signifies a beginning that ensures the survival of everything, the transmission of everything, except the "alive" and what was then presence has become absence or what has always been absence. We will not escape the sadness of the owl that Hegel was the first to feel, a grieving he eventually overcame. But is grief even possible? Through the blessing or fault of Hegel, we feel that what now seems so alive required the already dead. This is what Lyotard calls melancholy, and others call "nihilism."

But if the beginning is not the end, if we think of every birth as a death, and death as a birth without "truth," why is there a double nonbeing? Why is there nonbeing as birth and nonbeing as death?

It is an enigma, and the enigma of the beginning reveals that THERE IS [IL Y A] a relationship with what has no relationship. Birth that is not just melancholy, but is infinitely more painful than death. Thus, in *Poèmes de Samuel Wood*, des Forêts writes:

> *Tell yourself that at both ends of the journey*
> *The most wrenching pain is that of being born*
> *That lasts and clashes with the fear we have of dying,*
> *Tell yourself we aren't done with being born*
> *But the dead, the dead are done with dying.*

"Tell yourself." It's a story then, a story that I make up for myself or think I make up for myself, whereas it is told by others (but who is making up this story, if I am an abandoned child? And, according to Freud, I think I still am). This loss that comes to me from a story that abolishes the immediacy is the first suffering (supposing that we can keep count of them). But another suffering (still the same one, after all) is the memory of "*This nothingness country* [patrie néante] *whence I was unduly torn*" (*Les mégères de la mer* [Sea Shrews]). And yet another (but is it still the same one?):

> *Tell yourself we aren't done with being born*
> *But the dead, the dead are done with dying.*
> (*Poèmes de Samuel Wood*)

Thus, the demand of the beginning, which is extreme suffering, insofar as it is only a "maybe" (but an unquestionable illusion), threatened with annihilation without having been, or incapable of, being done with it, is far from the restorative death that Hegel lets us hope for.

Exigency, enigma.

The child, torn from his mother (from what he thought was an immediate union), who ends up delivering him prematurely (but if he is not big enough for existence in the world, he is too big for maternal immediacy, for the "motherland [*matrie*]"),[2] the child symbolizes the beginning of the period in between. He has surmounted the enigma of being-there, presenting others with the vivacity of a stupefying presence, but through this vivacity, EXPIATING it through disappointments, vain questions, silence at once obtained and lost. He is IN DEBT to the beginning (says Lyotard), and if he cannot acquit himself of this debt (since he cannot content himself with being an heir, even if he were son of a "king"), so he cannot stop himself from being born, birth SENTENCE [*arret de naissance* can mean either "birth warrant," a play on the phrase *arrêt de mort* or death sentence, or a stop to being born].

He seems, however, like "a sublime gift," "the sublime offering,"[3] but for OTHERS, not for himself, unless perhaps he is shot through with the enigma of the beginning as if by the lightning-flash about which he can never forget that it leaves him in the terror of blindness.

The ones they used to call an intractable boy

"Intractable" in himself or intractable because they called him that? And "intractable" (for those who said it) expressed either a blame, or a praise. And for himself he is no longer purely intractable, if he is so only in relation to those who say so.

There remains: Why be born? Why do we never come to an end of being born? Why, even beyond the end itself (and the end is indeed absolute nonbeing), is something left to us that is like a beginning? That is because the beginning is always first of all the capacity to judge, to say no to abjection (or to say yes or no), it is the POWER OF LIBERTY. The MATURE man who in the night sees himself judged by "the intractable boy," and judged as if he had compromised himself for not having completely kept his promise, is still precisely the one who keeps being born, born in the silent debt he continues to feel in relation to the lost nonbeing: to be born (not to be) [*naître/n'être*] without survival.

Unless one belongs to the world of the wise, says Samuel Wood. The wise man is Hegel's satisfied man, the one for whom there are no more questions, since he can expertly give an answer to everything, wanting, wishing, changing nothing else. He is dead without needing the Other (the other who accompanies and lends a hand until death). The Same absolutely the same.

But, for the non-Hegel, questions linger, words, silences, and also the glorious sun, the cries of birds, songs that escape the infernal necessity of language, jubilation of the creatures of the sky, music where, by anacrusis, the silence of what is still heard, or will be heard inside what is not heard, is sustained.

> *How many more times can one dream*
> *of a language*
> *Not subservient to words . . .*

. . . and not renounce the memory of the desire for *silent embraces* (what Levinas might call "caress").

That is said and it is barely said.

In *Les mégères de la mer*, there is this categorical assertion: *For being and no longer being are the same curse.* In *Poèmes de Samuel Wood*, the nonbeing from which we are born and the nonbeing in which we die also have a similar meaning and nonmeaning, with moreover the persistence, the continuation of absolute discontinuity.

In *Les mégères de la mer*:

> *And in my suffering memory which is my*
> *only possession . . .* ✗

Memory that, far from Proust, has no protection: *Nothing, having a memory of nothing, not even knowledge of one's death?*

And finally condemnation or abolition of the narrative [*récit*] that preserves no memorial of the journey from nonbeing to nonbeing.

> *But no memorial for the one who disavows*
> *his journey.*

In both poems (separated, however, by the disastrous Event), there is the same trial, or rather the interminable trial.

> *And in my suffering memory which is my only*
> *possession*
> *I look for where the child I was left his tracks.*

Tracks: traces not of what took place, but of what never happened. And that is what keeps us apart from Proust's memories, involuntary memories, gloriously grasped again and capable of distancing death by revived art.

More traces:

> Beneath the timeless arch where all-pure
>   nullity sits enthroned
> Even more absent by the very absence
>   of my traces . . .

There is a trial, however, a court appearance (*Les mégères de la mer* still) of the child with the child who has become other:

> There was for waking this evil torment of
>   childhood
> This other child smitten with the same secret
>   torment . . .

A confrontation that, without being repeated, takes the most incontestable form in *Poèmes de Samuel Wood* of the trial that is always old, always new.

It's because he sees with the eyes of conscience
The one they used to call an intractable boy
Coming back to judge the man who betrayed
    him.
Better to plead guilty than in the guise of defense
To pride oneself on an acquired wisdom

    (At the risk of accepting
the melancholy peace of Hegel.)

But why does the child torment him? Why does he make himself into a judge? It's because as a child, always still to be born, the power to judge and to be free still belongs to him, rejecting *the imposture of the tyrants of childhood.*

And it's also because the judge and the accused remain the same child, whose *judicial gaze* it is impossible *to soften* with *the heart* that *has not lost its young pride, its art that is to conceal its strong points, lucidity, its lofty place of pleasure* whence "he" (not knowing who "he" is) must begin again to hear, to pronounce the verdict.

We have not come to the end with age.

23

That is (once again) the enigma, the enigma of the strangeness of childhood—childhood that knows more about it because no answer suits it, articulating with a raised voice—the ravishing voice, ravished from the silence that still clings to it—the NON SERVIAM, the glorious refusal within the acquiescence of extreme distress.

Not wanting, not being able, to end, I will give myself over for the moment to the words of a Hassidic Master (who always refused to be Master), Rabbi Nachman of Breslav.

"It is forbidden to be old!"

Which we can understand first of all as: one is forbidden to reject being renewed, forbidden to confine oneself to an answer that would no longer pose the question—in the end (but there is no end) writing only to erase what has been written, or more precisely writing it by erasure itself, keeping exhaustion and the inexhaustible together: the DISAPPEARANCE that is never worn out.

So, he comes to write the secret Book only to burn it, becomes famous as the author of the "Burned Book."[4]

But perhaps that is the drawback of a mystic glory in which even without humbling himself or exalting himself he gives himself the possibility of a supreme ending.

I think Louis-René des Forêts refutes this possibility. The ultimate nonbeing cannot prevent birth from continuing, that is to say THERE IS always yet to be born, birth in debt to itself, to the silence it failed by taking a vow of it, but through which, even failed, the gift of grace and the grace of gift are maintained, laughter, tears, wildness, and perhaps finally CHANCE, but chance that has come after the fact and will not serve, precisely because it is chance only by concealing itself and refusing all use, all service.

Let us not forget that these poems are attributed to Samuel Wood. Is it a fiction to make someone else bear the responsibility for them, someone who would thus become the reality of the unreal? Is this another voice that the author hears only from time to time, or that he flees so that its secret will not be revealed, and so that the most profound, most disastrous truths remain unsaid? If there is never an absolute answer, but always perpetual questioning, I am still struck by certain almost calm moments when the negative does not triumph. For example in these three lines that seem to move away from the temptation of nihilism:

No, it is something otherwise obscure,
Tenderness that keeps the voice throttled
The duty of vigilant friendship.

And then the ten lines that are so striking, with an unequalled greatness of the "end," in which homage is made to *a voice come from elsewhere* (perhaps that of Samuel Wood or of the nameless) *inaccessible to time and erosion*; a voice that, even if it is also *illusory like a dream*, has *in it something that lasts / Even after its meaning has been lost.* And why? Because *its* TIMBRE (emphasis mine) *still quivers in the distance like a storm / We don't know if it's coming close or going.*

Voice, timbre, music. Is it through these words that the answerless question of the CONTRETEMPS [setback or difficulty—literally, a counter-time] opens up? Contretemps: even understood not subjectively, it can present itself to us under many forms. First of all Hegel once again, if with him we conceptually grasp the beginning only at the end and, in and through death, birth: a contretemps [counter-time] that then suppresses the immediacy of time and perhaps suppresses itself also in the melancholy of extreme satisfaction.

CONTRETEMPS: that is, differently perhaps, the anticipation of looking back through retrospection that gives the illusion of a present that has always already been lost, since it never existed.

Finally I will return to the mysterious, so poorly elucidated experience of Louis-René des Forêts of which I have given only a few glimpses. If in him the happiness and unhappiness of being born is always subjacent to the being who develops while thinking he distances himself from it, so much so that birth, endlessly continuing, is always beyond, we can consider the silence of the *infans* [infant, literally, the nonspeaking] to be always the precession of speech, just as nonbeing is not abolished in being, even if it seems to combine with it in the terrible come-and-go of THERE IS (being thinks it reclaims nonbeing, but birth in its nonbeing is so obstinate—*Ostinato*—without having yet surrendered its secret).

To resort to a term that dates back to Greek antiquity, but which has taken on a technical (albeit ill-defined) meaning during the nineteenth century, I will understand the experience (the contretemps) of Louis-René des Forêts as a sort of anacrusis. Anacrusis for the Greeks was a simple prelude, for instance on the lyre. In the examples from the nineteenth century, it becomes more complicated: at the inaugural open-ing of the measure, nothing is heard, or else a tone so weak it seems to fail and hence lasts without lasting, or longer than it lasts, so that after it or starting from it the note that is finally struck rises up to a some-times phenomenal burst, a burst or surge so strong it can only collapse—fall—into a new silence. Thus the before and the after displace each other and are not fixed in a determined place, without the practiced ear hearing there a confused jumble.

In this way the augural of the first or final childhood has undergone—in its first measure—a silence-cry, still animal and yet already human. He will preserve the emblem of this first silence (but was it the first? Hadn't there been in the antecedence of nonbeing—the nothingness fatherland or motherland—a silent communication, most intimate, most reserved?), a silence to which it is VOWED and out of which, by an impossible challenge, it makes a VOW. A silence that, in a concerted way, as in music, will here be inexplicably broken in the sublime fervor of a choral voice of such beauty (but this is no longer beauty) that silence forms again around it so that there is nothing more to be heard, just the voice in its dizzying ascen-sions, a silence, then, into which it falls back so absolutely that only in vain will it ever be sought again in the retroversion of the desperate memory.[5]

Whence the perhaps "demented" torment of an apparition to which disappearance was a prelude. An off-beat rhythm [*contretemps*] that the skill of the counterpart [*contrechant*] will imitate in vain.

Notes to "Anacrusis"

1. *Colloques sur Hannah Arendt*, Editions Tierce.

2. I refer here to Dominique Rabaté's excellent study: *Louis-René des Forêts: la voix et le volume*, Paris: Ed. José Corti.

3. Cf. Jean-Luc Nancy, *Le Sublime*, Paris: Belin.

4. Cf. the book by Marc-Alain Ouaknin with the same title, *Le Livre brûlé* (Ed. Lieu Commun), a book that not only deals with Hassidic literature, but also constitutes a remarkable introduction to the study of the Talmud.

5. In spoken song (*Sprachgesang*) we find, especially in our era, that in the vocal attack, the first note is produced/not produced, since the lips remain closed; for the second, the mouth scarcely opens, starting and stopping like a breath; the third note, which coincides with the first word of the poem, is also the first to be sung, emerging with all the more force since it is first to leave the nonmusical sphere. So there was something like a reticence (a shame?) to be sung, to reconcile song and word and the

"speech with mouth closed," still a silence and a silence that is intoned, is made timbre in the voice. Similarly in *Une mémoire démentielle*, the child of the chorus, without abandoning his silence, sings at first only without singing, sings "from the tip of his lips," merely miming the vocal effort, till the moment when he lets himself be carried off in the song by a dizzying escalade, a raging wind, a dazzling speed that reaches a height that surpasses the very heavens, until the suspense that culminates in the end.

The Beast of Lascaux

I would like to recall that this text was first published in book form by G. L. M. in 1958. Today, its republication would like, not to abolish, but to restore by means of a fleeting memory, like a double homage to friendship—of René Char, and of Guy Levis Mano— what comes to us from poetry, as if from a forever passing eternity.

—M. B.

The Unnamable Beast

The unnamable Beast brings up the rear of the
    graceful herd, like a comic Cyclops.
Eight jibes form its adornment, divide its madness.
The Beast belches piously into the rustic air.
Its swollen, drooping flanks are painful, will soon
    empty themselves of their fullness.
From its hoofs to its vain tusks, it is surrounded
    by fetor.

Thus appears to me in the frieze at Lascaux,
    fantastically disguised mother:
Wisdom, her eyes full of tears.

                         —René Char

In the *Phaedrus*, Plato discusses a strange language, in
order to condemn it: someone speaks and yet no one
is speaking; it is indeed speech, but it does not think

what it says, and it always says the same thing, incapable of choosing its interlocutors, incapable of replying if they question it, or of coming to its own aid if they attack it: its fate condemns it to being bandied about, abandons it to chance, and condemns truth to being the offspring of chance. Entrusting it with the truth is actually entrusting it to death. Thus Socrates proposes that we should distance ourselves as much as possible from this speech, as if from a dangerous disease, and that we confine ourselves to the real language, which is spoken language, in which speech is sure of finding a living guarantee in the presence of the one who utters it.

Written speech = dead speech, speech of oblivion. This extreme mistrust of writing, also shared by Plato, shows what doubts the new use of written communication could give rise to, what problems could appear: what is this speech [parole] that doesn't have behind it the personal guarantee of a real person, concerned with truth? The already belated humanism of Socrates is here equidistant from two worlds of which he is fully aware, and which he rejects with vigorous decisiveness. The first is the impersonal knowledge of a book that doesn't demand to be guaranteed by the thinking of one person alone, and is never true, for it can only become a truth in the world of everyone, through the very advent of that world. Such a knowledge is linked to the development of technique in all forms and it turns speech, and writing, into a technique.

But Socrates, who rejects the impersonal knowledge of the book, rejects no less forcefully—but with more reverence—another impersonal language, the pure speech that seeks to articulate the sacred. We are no longer, he says, the kind of people who are content to listen to the voice of the oak or the stone. "You others, you moderns, want to know who it is who is speaking, and what country he comes from." So that everything that is said against writing would serve, as well, to discredit the recited speech of the hymn, where the speaker, whether he is the poet or the echo of the poet, is nothing more than the irresponsible organ of a language that infinitely surpasses him.

In that way, mysteriously, although writing is linked to the development of prose, when verse stops being an indispensable tool for memory, the written thing seems essentially close to sacred speech, whose strangeness it seems to carry into the written work, and whose excessiveness, risk, and power that evades all calculation and refuses any guarantee, it inherits.

Like sacred speech, what is written comes from no one knows where, it is authorless, without origin, and, hence, refers to something more original. Behind the written word, no one is present, but it gives voice to absence, just as in the oracle where the divine speaks, the god himself is never present in his speech, and it is the absence of god that speaks then. And the oracle doesn't justify itself, or explain itself, or defend itself, any more than writing does: no dialogue with the written, and no dialogue with the god. Socrates is still astonished by this silence that speaks.

Faced with the strangeness of the written work, Socrates' unease is finally the same that he experiences when faced with the work of art, whose unusual essence inspires his mistrust, if not scorn: "The terrible thing about writing, Phaedrus, is its resemblance to painting: Don't the by-products of painting present themselves as living beings, but aren't they majestically silent when one questions them?" What strikes him, then, what seems "terrible" to him, in writing as well as in painting, is the silence, a majestic silence, a silence that is inhuman in itself, that makes the shudder of sacred energies pass into art, those forces that, through horror and terror, open man up to alien regions.

There is nothing more impressive than this astonishment before the silence of art, this unease of the lover of words, of the man faithful to the honesty of living speech: what is this that has the immutability of eternal things and yet is nothing but appearance, that says true things, but behind which is only emptiness, the impossibility of speaking, so that here the real has nothing to sustain it, seems baseless, is the scandal of what *seems* real, but is only image and, through image and semblance, draws truth into the abysses where there is no truth, or meaning, or even error? That is why Plato and Socrates hasten, in the same passage, to make both writing and art into a pasttime, where the serious is not compromised, an amusement that will be reserved for hours of recreation, like those miniature artificial gardens grown in baskets to adorn celebrations, called "gardens of Adonis." Written speech, the "volume," will thus be nothing but a "garden of written letters," capable at the very most of commemorating the works or achievements of knowledge, without having any part in the work of their discovery. And here we see Socrates once again establishing a connection between writing and the sacred by comparing it to the celebration that interrupts man's laborious activity devoted to reality in order to initiate it into the time where gods and men meet each other: the time of celebration. But the ancient prophetic wildness of the oak is now nothing but the pleasant miniature garden, just as the celebration is now only an amusement.

We sometimes wonder why René Char, a poet linked with our destiny, feels intimately close to the name of Heraclitus, whose victorious figure, whose "solar eagle's sight," "proud, stable, anxious genius,"[1] he himself evokes, but who is also evoked, brought before us, with a more immediate reminder, by so many of his works, shards of poem where the poem seems reduced to the sharp edge of pure brilliance, to the cut of a decision.

Perhaps the beginning of an answer can be given us by two thoughts of Heraclitus. Heraclitus responds in a way to Socrates by recognizing the true authority of language in what makes the impersonal speech of the oracle a danger and a scandal: "The Lord whose oracle is at Delphi neither reveals nor hides anything, but indicates." Here the word "indicates" reflects its root image—the index finger—and makes the word into the silently pointing finger, the "index finger whose nail is torn out," which, saying nothing, hiding nothing, opens up space, opens it up to whoever is open to this arrival. Socrates is undoubtedly right: what he wants is not a language that says nothing, behind which nothing is hidden, but a sure speech, guaranteed by a presence: one that can be exchanged, one that is made for exchange. The speech in which he trusts is always the speech of some thing and the language of some one, both of them already revealed and present, never a beginning speech. And, hence, deliberately, with a prudence we shouldn't misconstrue, he renounces any language that is oriented toward the origin, renounces the oracle as well as the work of art by which a voice is given to the beginning, by which a summons is addressed to an initial decision.

The language in which the origin speaks is essentially prophetic. That does not mean that it dictates future events; it means that it does not rely on something that already exists—neither on an already accepted truth nor on a language that has already been spoken or verified. It announces, because it begins. It *indicates* the future, because it does not yet speak: language of the future, insofar as it, itself, is already like a future language, which anticipates itself, finding its meaning and legitimacy only ahead of itself, that is to say fundamentally unjustified. And it is the unreasonable wisdom of the Sibyl, who makes herself heard for a thousand years, since she is never heard now, and this language that opens up duration, which rends and begins, without smiling, without ornament and without makeup, nakedness of first speech: "The Sibyl who, from a foaming mouth, utters words that are unattractive, unadorned and unpainted, makes her oracles resound for a thousand years, for it is the god who inspires her."

If we found it useful to sketch with a few lines the force of the poem as it comes to light in the work of René Char, we could be content with saying that it is this future speech, impersonal and always yet to come, where, in the decision of a beginning language, what is at stake in the fate that is closest and most immediate to us is nonetheless intimately spoken to us. It is, in the fullest sense, the song of presentment, of promise and awakening—not that Char sings of what will be tomorrow, or that in his work a future, happy or unhappy, is precisely revealed to us—but, in the space presentment holds, he firmly links speech to flight and, through the flight of speech, he firmly lays hold of the coming of a wider horizon, the affirmation of a first day. The future is rare, and every day that comes is not a day that begins. Even rarer is speech that, in its silence, is the reserve of a speech yet to come, which turns us, even if it's close to our finish, toward the force of the beginning. In each of René Char's works, we hear poetry utter the pledge that, with anxiety and in uncertainty, joins it to its own future, forces it to speak only starting from this future, to give, in advance, to this coming, the firmness and promise of its speech.

In *Moulin premier*: "In the course of his searches, the poet sometimes runs aground on a shore where he wasn't expected till much later, after his annihilation." In *Partage formel*: "To each collapse of the evidence the poet responds with a salvo of the future." In *Le Poème pulvérisé*: "Poetry, the future life inside the retrained man." In *Les Matineaux*, the title of which is already a summons to the "First arisen": "Conquest and indefinite preservation of that conquest *ahead of us* that murmurs our shipwreck, diverts our disappointment." Or again, in one of his recent works, this kind of somber conclusion: "I am now not very far from the line where things fit together, and from the final instant when, after everything in my mind, through fusion and synthesis, has become absence and promise of a future that does not belong to me, I will pray you to grant me my silence and my leave."[2]

Denouement in the future silence whence, precisely, the unsettling movements of the poem entitled "Lettera amorosa" rise up today, where the space and freedom of love, the loving intimacy of the poet, are made present to us with the simplicity of words intact; and despite appearances, it is indeed still poetry that is speaking to us here about itself, that is speaking to us, under the face of passion, about its always future essence, its fervor always to come in its most real, most burning present: in that it is linked to desire, which is, like it, the effervescence of the whole future in the burning of the instant; it is eternally joined to it, as the lines from *Seuls demeurent* say— "The poem is the realized love of desire that has remained desire"—and as the pages of "Lettera amorosa" confirm, where it seems that poetry wants to grasp, behind light, the violent opening, the most primal jagged cut by which everything is illumined and awakens and is promised: "The whole mouth and the hunger of something better than light (more jagged and more grasping) explode."[3]

But those are only reference points. Or rather: poem in which the poem is as if still to come, in

which a promise is drawn up, the decision of a beginning, and so it contains this sometimes brief speech,
which could be called restrained, if it didn't preserve
so well the prodigality, the plenitude, and generosity
of the source. "*Lord Time! Wild grass! Powerful walk-
ers!*" Speech that does not repeat itself, that does not
make use of itself, that does not say things already
present, that is not the tireless come-and-go of Socratic
dialogue, but speech like that of the Lord of Delphi,
speech that is the voice that has said nothing yet,
that wakes and awakens, a voice that is sometimes
harsh and demanding, that comes from afar and summons afar.

So comes it that, in the firmness that draws it
up and maintains it in constant insurrection, it links
the poem to the greatest risk, it entrusts it to this risk,
and this confidence in "the considerable danger," by
which our own situation is clarified, appoints poetry
to the adventure it must essentially be, when it exposes itself, without guarantee and without certainty,
to the freedom of what is still only yet to come.

Dense speech, closed in on its own anxiety,
that calls out to us and drags us ahead, so that it
sometimes seems to join poetry to ethics, and to tell
us what is expected of us, but that is because it is itself

this injunction that is the form of every beginning. Every beginning speech, although it is the gentlest and most secret impulse, is, because it moves us infinitely forward, one that upsets and demands the most: like the most tender break of day in which all the violence of a first clarity is declared, and like oracular speech that dictates nothing, forces nothing on us, that does not even speak, but makes this silence into the finger imperiously pointing toward the unknown.

When the unknown beckons us, when speech borrows its voice from the oracle where nothing actual speaks, but which forces one who listens to tear himself from his present to come to himself as if to what does not yet exist, this speech is often intolerant, of a haughty violence that, in its rigor and through its unarguable verdict, takes us away from ourselves by ignoring us. Prophets and visionaries speak with a sovereignty that is all the more abrupt when what speaks in them ignores them: this ignorance that makes them timid makes them authoritarian and gives their voice more hardness than brilliance.

It is the chance of the poem to be able to escape prophetic intolerance, and it is this chance that, with a purity of which we are scarcely aware, the work of René Char offers us—a work that speaks to us from so far away, but with an intimate comprehension that brings it so close to us. This work has the force of the impersonal, but it is to the faithfulness of a unique destiny that it summons us, a tense but patient work, tempestuous and still, energetic, concentrated in on itself, in the explosive brevity of the instant, a power of image and affirmation that "pulverizes" the poem and yet keeps the slowness, the continuity, and the understanding of the uninterrupted.

Where does that come from? It is because it speaks the beginning, but through the long, patient, silent approach of the origin, in the profound life of everything, welcoming everything. Nature is powerful throughout this work, and nature here is not just solid earthly things—sun, water, the wisdom of the enduring peoples; it is not even all things, or universal plenitude, or the infinity of the cosmos, but what is already before "everything," the immediate and the faraway, what is more real than all real things and what is forgotten in each thing, the link that cannot link, by which everything, the whole, is tied together. In the work of René Char, nature is this testing of the origin, and it is through that trial, where it is exposed to the emergence of an umlimited freedom and to the profundity of the absence of time, that poetry experiences awakening and, becoming beginning speech, becomes the speech of the beginning, the one that is the pledge of the future. That is why it is not the anticipation that, in a provocative way, would rush prophetically into time and would fix, bind the future; nor is it the speech of the seer, in the "deranged" manner of Rimbaud, but it is "foreseeing," like what reserves and safeguards, what assures and acclimates profound life and the free communication of everything, speech in which the origin becomes a beginning. "The great foreseers precede a climate, sometimes determine it, but do not anticipate actions. At the most, they can deduce them from this climate, pencil in the outlines of their phantom, and, if they have qualms, by anticipation, blur them. What will take place bathes, in the same way as what has happened, in a kind of immersion." "But who will re-establish around us this immensity, this density actually made for us, which, from all sides, not divinely, used to bathe us?" (À une Sérénité crispée.)[4]

If the speech of the poem in René Char's work evokes the speech of thought in Heraclitus, as it is has been handed down to us, it would seem that we owe that to this relationship with the origin, a relationship found in both Char and Heraclitus, not entirely confident or stable, but fraught and tempestuous. Xenophanes, probably younger than Heraclitus, but like him one of those whom Plato (with a slightly mocking tenderness) called the Old Ones, was one of those wandering bards, going from country to country and living on their songs; but what sang in his song was already thought, a speech that rejected the legends of the gods, questioned them fiercely and questioned itself, so that those who listened to him were witnesses to this very strange event: the birth of philosophy in the poem.

There is, in the experience of art and in the genesis of the work, a moment where the work is still nothing but an indistinct violence tending to open up and tending to close, tending to exalt in a space that opens up and tending to withdraw into the profundity of dissimulation: the work is then the struggling intimacy of irreconcilable and inseparable moments, communication torn between the measure of the work that established a certain power and the measurelessness or excess of the work that strives toward impossibility, between form where it grasps hold of itself and limitlessness where it rejects itself, between work as beginning and the origin on the basis of which there is never any work, where the eternal absence of work [*désoeuvrement*] reigns. This antagonistic exaltation is what founds communication, and it is this exaltation that will finally take the personified shape of the demand to read and the demand to write. The language of thought and the language that is used in poetic song are like the different directions this original dialogue has taken, but, in both of them, and every time they both renounce their appeased form and move back up toward their source, it seems that this more original strife of more indistinct demands begins anew, in a more or less "lively" way, and one can say that any poetic work, in the course of its genesis, is a return to this initial struggle and even, so long as it is a work, that it does not stop being the intimacy of its eternal birth.

In the work of René Char, as well as in fragments of Heraclitus, it is this eternal genesis we are witnessing from instant to instant, this fierce combat with what is previous, where the transparency of thought comes to light through the obscure image that retains it, where speech itself, suffering a twofold violence, seems to be illumined by the naked silence of thought, seems to thicken, to be filled with an eloquent, incessant profundity, a murmuring where nothing lets itself be heard. Voice of the oak, rigorous and closed language of aphorism, that is how, in the indistinctness of a first speech, the *"mother fantastically disguised, Wisdom, her eyes full of tears"* speaks to us, whom René Char, looking at the frieze at Lascaux, identified as the figure of *"the unnamable Beast."*[5] Strange wisdom, too ancient for Socrates yet also too new, from which, however, despite the unease that made him distance himself from it, we must think that he is not excluded, he who accepted as a guarantee of speech only the presence of a living person, and who nonetheless came to die from it, in order to keep his word.

Notes

1. Foreword to *Héraclite d'Éphèse*, new French translation by Yves Battistini, Éditions Cahiers d'Art.

2. *À une Sérénité crispée*, Gallimard, 1951.

3. *Lettera amorosa*, Gallimard, 1953.

4. *Partage formel* sheds light on this "immensity" of "immersion," which is the very space of song and in which everything lives, thus: "In poetry, it is only starting from communication and the free disposition of the totality of things among themselves through us, that we find ourselves involved and defined, so that we can obtain our original form and our preliminary properties."

5. *La Paroi et la Prairie*, Paris: G. L. M., 1952.

The Last to Speak

Plato: *For of death, no one has knowledge*, and Paul Celan: *No one bears witness for the witness*. And yet, always, we choose a companion for ourselves: not for ourselves, but for something inside us, outside us, that needs us to be lacking for ourselves in order to pass the line we will not reach. Companion lost in advance, the very loss that is henceforth in our place.

Where can we look for the witness for whom there is no witness?

ein ins Stumme entglittenes
Ich
   [Vol. I of the Suhrkamp *Gesammelte Schriften*, p. 156]

an I escaped into silence

Wieder Begegnungen mit
vereinzelten Worten wie:
Steinschlag, Hartgräser, Zeit.
   [I, 192]

Again encounters with
isolated words like:
stonefall, hard reeds, time.

dass bewahrt sei
ein durchs Dunkel
getragenes Zeichen,
   [I, 159]

What is speaking to us here reaches us through the extreme tension of language, its concentration, the necessity to maintain, to carry one toward the other, in a union that does not create unity, words hence-forth associated, yoked for something other than their meaning, only oriented toward——. And what is speaking to us, in these poems that are often very short, where words and phrases seem, by the rhythm of their undefined brevity, surrounded with white space, is that this white space, these stops, these silences, are not pauses or intervals that allow the reader to breathe, but belong to the same rigor, one that authorizes only a little relaxation, a nonverbal rigor that is not sup-posed to convey meaning, as if the void were less a lack than a saturation, an emptiness saturated with emptiness. But still it is not there I would concentrate first, but on the fact that such a language, often so hard (as in some late poems of Hölderlin), not hard—something strident, a shrill sound beyond what can become song—never comes to produce a language of violence, does not strike the other, is not animated by any aggressive or destructive intention: as if the de-struction of self had already taken place so that the other is preserved, or so that *a sign borne by obscurity is maintained.*

mit der untrüglichen Spur:

. . . in der Dünung
wandernder Worte
  [I, 204]

Gras, auseinandergeschrieben
  [I, 197]

Lies nicht mehr—schau!
Schau nicht mehr—geh!
  [I, 197]

Toward what does this language tend? *Sprach-gitter*: would speaking be staying behind the bars—the bars of a prison—through which the freedom of the outside is promised (or refused): snow, night, the place that has a name, that does not have a name; or might speaking instead be thinking oneself provided with these bars, which makes one hope there might be something to decipher and, thence, to enclose oneself again in the illusion that meaning or truth might be free, over there, in the landscape where *the trace does not deceive*? But, just as writing is read in the form of a thing, of the outside of a thing condensing into such or such a thing, not to designate it, but to be written there *in the swelling movement of words that are always going,* isn't the outside also read as a writing, writing without link, always already outside itself: *grass, written outside one another*? Perhaps the recourse—is it a recourse, an appeal?—is to confide itself, beyond the network of language (*eye, circle of eye between the bars*), in the wait for a wider gaze, a possibility of seeing, seeing without even the words that signify sight:

> *do not read—look!*
> *Do not look—go!*

59

Zur Blindheit über—
redete Augen.
  [I, 226]

Augen weltblind,
Augen im Sterbegeklüft,
Augen Augen:
  [I, 168]

Geh, deine Stunde
hat keine Schwestern, du bist—
bist zuhause.
  [I, 197]

Sight, then (maybe), but always in *sight* of a movement, associated with a movement: as if it were a
question of going toward the summons of these eyes
that see beyond what there is to see: *eyes blind to the
world, eyes that speech submerges to the point of blindness,* that look (or have their place) *in the series of
fissures of dying.*

> *Eyes blind to the world,*
> *Eyes in the crevasses of dying,*
> *Eyes eyes:*
> *Do not read—look!*
> *Do not look—go!*

Movement without aim. Hour that is always the last:

> *Go, your hour*
> *has no sisters, you are—*
> *are there, returned.*

Movement, though, that is not interrupted: the assertion of return just makes it more sterile, the slow
movement of the wheel turning by itself and on itself,
rays on a blackish field, perhaps night, the nocturnal
wheel of stars, but

die Nacht
braucht keine Sterne, nirgends
fragt es nach dir.
    [I, 197]

Das umhergestossene
Immer—Licht, lehmgelb,
hinter
Planetenhäuptern.

Erfundene
Blicke, Seh -
narben,
ins Raumschiff gekerbt,
betteln um Erden—
münder.
    [II, 71]

night
has no need of stars,

just as

nowhere
is there any asking for you.

The outside: there where eyes are focused—
eyes detached from the person, eyes one could think
are solitary and impersonal:

incessant light, silt yellow,
here there shifted
behind the major planets.

Looks
invented, scars
to see,
carved in the vessel of space,
eyes

that, disembodied, deprived of any ability to commu-
nicate, wandering,

beg for earthly
mouths.

ERBLINDE schon heute:
auch die Ewigkeit steht voller Augen—
  [II, 45]

Unverhüllt an den Toren des Traumes
streitet ein einsames Aug.
  [I, 26]

Es wird noch ein Aug sein,
ein fremdes, neben
dem unsern: stumm
unter steinernem Lid.
  [I, 153]

O dieses trunkene Aug,
das hier umherirrt wie wir
und uns zuweilen
staunend in eins schaut.
  [I, 118]

Eyes that stud eternity (*eternity rises up full of eyes*);
hence perhaps the wish to blind oneself:

> *BLIND YOURSELF beginning today:*
> *even eternity is full of eyes*

→ 73
81

But depriving oneself of sight is also a way of
seeing. The obsession with eyes designates something
besides the visible.

> *Open to the gates of dream*
> *struggles a solitary eye.*

> *There will be, next to our own,*
> *another eye,*
> *foreign: silent*
> *beneath the eyelid of stone.*

> *O this drunken eye*
> *that all around like us*
> *wanders here and sometimes*
> *surprised looks singly at us.*

Eräugtes
Dunkel darin.

Augen und Mund stehn so offen und leer, Herr.
  [I, 158]

Dein Aug, so blind wie der Stein.

Blume—ein Blindenwort.
  [I, 164]

Gesänge:
Augenstimmen, im Chor,
  [I, 169]

Du bist,
wo dein Aug ist, du bist
oben, bist
unten, ich
finde hinaus.
  [I, 219]

In der Luft, da bleibt deine Wurzel, da,
in der Luft.
  [I, 290]

Darkness there
struck with force by the eye.

Eyes and mouth, so open and so empty, Lord.

Your eye, as blind as a stone.

Flower—a blind man's word.

Songs:
voice of gazes, in the choir,
You are,
there where your eye is, you are
up high, are
down low, I
turn toward the outside.

The relationship with the outside, never already given, attempt at movement or progress, relationship without attachments and without roots—this is not just indicated by the empty transcendence of empty eyes, but asserted explicitly by Paul Celan in

In the air, there remains your root, there,
in the air.

wir schaufeln ein Grab in den Lüften da
liegt man nicht eng
    [III, 63]

we dig a grave in the skies
we won't be cramped there

draussen bei
den andern Welten.
    [I, 287]

outside near
other worlds.

. . . hinaus
in Unland und Unzeit . . .
    [I, 287]

. . . outside
in no-country and no-time
    (the counter-time) . . .

Weiss,
was sich uns regt,
ohne Gewicht,
was wir tauschen.
Weiss und Leicht:
lass es wandern.
    [I, 165]

White,
what moves for us,
weightless,
what we exchange.
White, Light:
let it wander.

his prose fragments as his possibility: to speak with things. *We are, when we speak thus with things, always in the process of questioning them to know where they come from and where they are going, a question always open, endless, indicating the Open, the empty, the free— there where we are far outside. It is this place that the poem looks for also.*

This outside that is not nature—or at least not the nature still spoken of by Hölderlin—even if it is associated with space, planets, and stars, with a sometimes brilliant cosmic sign, the outside of the faraway, a still loving faraway, reaches us through words that return with insistence (chosen perhaps by the attraction of our reading)—*Schnee, Ferne, Nacht, Asche* [snow, distance, night, ashes]—that return as if to make us believe in a relationship with a reality or matter that is powdery, soft, light, perhaps welcoming, but such an impression is soon turned toward the aridity of *stone* (a word that is almost always there), of *chalk*, of *limestone* and *gravel* (*Kreide, Kalk, Kiesel*), snow whose sterile whiteness is the always whiter white (crystal, crystal), without increase or growth: the white that is at the bottom of what is bottomless:

69

Flügelnacht, weither gekommen und nun
für immer gespannt
über Kreide und Kalk.
Kiesel, abgrundhin rollend.
Schnee. Une mehr noch des Weissen.
   [I, 128]

Augen, weltblind, im Sterbegeklüft: Ich komm,
Hartwuchs im Herzen.
Ich komm.
   [I, 128]

die Welt, ein Tausendkristall
The world, multiple crystal

Atemkristall
breath crystal
   [I, 202]

Das Schneebett unter uns beiden, das Schneebett.
Kristall um Kristall,
zeittief gegittert, wir fallen,
wir fallen und liegen und fallen.

Night shaped like a wing, come from afar and now
forever stretched
above chalk and limestone.
Flint, rolling down to the abyss.
Snow. And always more White.

Schneebett bed of snow: the gentleness of this designation introduces nothing that might console:

Eyes, blind to the world, in the
crevasses of dying: I am coming,
A hard growth in my heart.
I am coming.

Attraction, appeal of falling. But the *I* is not alone, it goes on to *we*, and this two-person fall unites, into the present, even what falls:

The bed of snow beneath us
two, the bed of snow.
Crystal surrounded by crystal,
interlaced in the profundity of
time, we fall,
we fall and lie down and fall.

Und fallen:
Wir waren. Wir sind.
Wir sind ein Fleisch mit der Nacht.
In den Gängen, den Gängen.
[I, 168]

DU DARFST mich getrost
mit Schnee bewirten:
   [II, 11]

ICH KANN DICH NOCH SEHN:
ein Echo,
ertastbar mit Fühl -
wörtern, am Abschieds -
grat.
Dein Gesicht scheut leise,
wenn es auf einmal
lampenhaft hell wird
in mir, an der Stelle,
wo man am schmerzlichsten Nie sagt.
   [II, 275]

And fall:
We were. We are.
We are, flesh and night, together.
In the avenues, in the avenues.

YOU CAN *without fear*
feed me on snow:

This two-person fall marks the always oriented, magnetized relationship that nothing could break and that solitude still bears:

I CAN STILL SEE YOU: echo
that can be reached by the palpation
of words, on the edge of
Farewell.
Your face gently shy,
When all of a sudden
a lamplight is created
in me, in the place
where they say with the greatest pain Never.

Pain that is only pain, without claim or resentment:

(Auf dem senkrechten
Atemseil, damals,
höher als oben,
zwischen zwei Schmerzknoten, während
der blanke
Tatarenmond zu uns heraufklomm,
grub ich mich in dich und in dich.)
   [II, 72]

(Wär ich wie du. Wärst du wie ich.
Standen wir nicht
unter einem Passat?
Wir sind Fremde.)
Ich bin du, wenn ich ich bin.
   [I, 167]

I am you, when I am I.

(On the vertical cord
of breath, then,
higher than on high,
between two knots of pain, while
up to us heaved the
white Tartar moon,
in you and in you I buried myself.)

All that is in parentheses, as if the interval reserved
a thought that, there where everything is absent, is
also a gift, a memory, an influence in common:

(If I were like you. If you were
like me.
Wouldn't we have stayed standing
together in one single oncoming wind?
We are strangers.)

Wir sind Fremde: strangers, but both strangers, having
still to bear in common this wandering of distance
that holds us absolutely apart. *We are strangers.* Just
as, if there is silence, two silences fill our mouths:

zwei
Mundvoll Schweigen.

75

Also
stehen noch Tempel. Ein
Stern
hat wohl noch Licht.
Nichts,
nichts ist verloren.

Ho-
sianna.
   [I, 204]

. . . das hundert-
züngige Mein-
Gedicht, das Genicht.
   [II, 31]

. . . mine—poem
with a hundred tongues, no after no.

Let us remember that, if we can: *two mouthfuls of silence.*

Can one say then that poetic assertion, in Paul Celan (always perhaps distanced from hope as it is distanced from truth—but always in motion toward both) still leaves something, if not to hope for, then to think about, through brief phrases that suddenly illumine, even after everything has sunk into darkness: *night has no need of stars (. . .) a star still certainly has light.*

> *Thus*
> *temples are still standing. A*
> *star*
> *still certainly has light.*
> *Nothing,*
> *nothing is lost.*
> *Ho-*
> *sanna.*

So even if we utter the uppercase word Nothing, in the abrupt hardness it has in the original language, it is possible to add: nothing is lost, so that nothing is perhaps articulated with loss. Whereas the Hebraic

Ja.
Orkane, Par-
tikelgestöber, es blieb
Zeit, blieb,
es beim zu versuchen—er
war gastlich, er
fiel nicht ins Wort. Wie
gut wir es hatten:
   [I, 201]

SINGBARER REST . . .

—Entmündigte Lippe, melde,
dass etwas geschieht, noch immer,
unweit von dir.
   [II, 36]

cry of jubilation is divided to begin with a groan. And here again:

> Yes.
> Hurricanes, par-
> ticles whirling, there was
> time remaining, remaining
> to test near the stone—it
> was hospitable, it
> does not forbid speech. How
> happy we were:

Or elsewhere:

> REST (remainder) SINGABLE

with this kind of finale:

> Forbidden lip,
> announce
> that something is still arriving,
> not far from you.

Phrase written with a terrible simplicity, fated to remain in us in the uncertainty where it remains, *dieses*

Brot kauen, mit

Schreibzähnen.

   [II, 358]

O diese wandernde leere

gästliche Mitte. Getrennt,

fall ich dir zu, fällst

du mir zu,

   [I, 219]

Ein Nichts

waren wir, sind wir, werden

wir bleiben, blühend:

die Nichts-, die

Niemandsrose.

   [I, 225]

. . .   Es ist,

ich weiss es, nicht wahr,

bearing, interlaced, the movement of hope and the immobility of distress, the demand of the impossible, for it is from the forbidden, from the forbidden alone, that what there is to say can come: *this bread to chew with the teeth of writing.*

Yes, even there where Nothing reigns, even when separation does its work, the relationship is not broken, even if it is interrupted.

> *O this wandering center hospitable*
> *void. Separated,*
> *I fall in you, you fall*
> *in me . . .*
>
> *A nothing*
> *we were, are, will*
> *remain, in flower:*
> *from nothing the rose,*
> *no one's rose.*

And this, which we must again receive in its hard-ness:

> *. . .*   *It is,*
> *I know, not true,*

dass wir lebten, es ging
blind nur ein Atem zwischen
Dort und Nicht-da und Zuweilen, (...)
ich weiss,
ich weiss und du weisst, wir wussten,
wir wussten nicht, wir
waren ja da und nicht dort,
und zuweilen, wenn
nur das Nichts zwischen uns stand, fanden
wir ganz zueinander.
   [I, 217]

Sichtbares, Hörbares, das
frei-
werdende Zeltwort:
Mitsammen.
   [I, 257]

Augen, weltblind, im Sterbegeklüft:
Ich komm,
Hartwuchs im Herzen.
Ich komm.

Die Nacht besamt, als könnt es
noch andere geben, nächtiger als
diese.
   [II, 333]

that we lived, only
a breath passed blind between
there and not-there and sometimes . . .
I know,
I know and you know, we knew,
we did not know, we
were indeed there and not over there, and sometimes,
provided that between us
Nothing rose up, completely,
we found ourselves
joined to each other.

So that in the journey through the desert (the anabasis), there remains, always, as if to take shelter there, a free word, that one can see, hear: *be together.*

Eyes, to the world blind, in the series
of fissures of dying: I am coming,
A hard growth in my heart.
I am coming.

Fascinated, I reread these words, themselves always inscribed under fascination. In the depths of the depths, in the mine of the beyond (*In der Jenseits-Kaue*), there is night, the night that spreads and scatters as if there

Tief

in der Zeitenschrunde,

beim

Wabeneis wartet, ein Atemkristall,

dein unumstössliches

Zeugnis.
  [II, 31]

Deep

in the crevasse of time,

near the honeycombed ice

waits, breathcrystal,

your unimpeachable

testimony.

Sprich auch du,
sprich als letzter,
sag deinen Spruch.

. . . *der Tod ist ein Meister aus Deutschland*
  [I, 42]

. . . death, a master come from Germany

("Todesfuge" [Death Fugue])

84

were yet another night, more nocturnal than this one. There is night, but, in the night, also eyes—eyes?—scars in place of sight, they summon, they attract, so that one must respond: *I am coming*, I am coming with a hard growth in my heart. Where should I come? Come, even if it's nowhere, only there where—in the fissures-crevasses of dying—the incessant light (which does not illumine) fascinates. *Im Sterbegeklüft*. Not one single rift or fissure, but an indefinite succession—series—of crevasses, something that opens up and does not open up or that opens up, always already closed again, and not the gaping of the abyss where one would only have to slide into the immense, unfathomable void, but rather those clefts or fissures whose narrow constraint, the narrowness of failing, seizes us, by an impossible breaking through, without allowing us to plummet in a freefall, even if it is eternal: that perhaps is dying, the hard growth in the heart of dying, the witness without witness to whom Celan has given a voice, uniting him *with the night-drenched voices, voice when there is no more voice, only a belated rustling, foreign to hours, offered as a present to every thought.*

Death, speech. In the prose fragments where Celan states his poetic design, never does he exactly

Celan

renounce a design. In his Bremen speech: *Poems are always on the move, they are in relation to something, tending toward something. Toward what? Toward something that keeps itself open and that could be inhabited, toward a You to whom one might be able to speak, toward a reality close to speech.* It is in this same brief oration that, with an extreme simplicity and sobriety, Celan alludes to what it meant for him—and, through him, for us—not to have this possibility of writing poems taken away, poems written in a language through which death bore down on him, on those near to him, on the millions of Jews and non-Jews, an event without response. *Accessible, close and not lost, there remained, in the middle of everything he had to lose, this single thing: language. It, language, remained not lost, yes, despite everything. But it then had to go through its own absences of response, go through a terrible silence, go through the thousand thick obscurities of a deadly speech. This speech went through them without giving itself words for what had taken place. But it went through this place of the Event. Went through it and could once again return one day,* enriched by all that. *It is in this language that, during these years and the years that followed, I tried to write poems: in order to speak, in order to orient myself and learn where I was and where I had to go for some reality to take shape for me. It*

Sprich auch du,
sprich als letzter,
sag deinen Spruch.

Sprich—
Doch scheide das Nein nicht vom Ja.
Gib deinem Spruch auch den Sinn:
gib ihm den Schatten.

Gib ihm Schatten genug,
gib ihm so viel,
als du um dich verteilt weisst zwischen
Mittnacht und Mittag und Mittnacht.

was, we can see, event, movement, progress, it was the attempt to reach a direction.

Speak, you too, even if you are the last to speak. That is what a poem—and perhaps we are now better prepared to understand it—gives us to read, gives us to live, allowing us to grasp in it this movement of poetry as Celan offered it to us, almost ironically: *Poetry, Ladies and Gentlemen: that speech of the infinite, speech of hollow death and of Nothing alone.* Let us read this poem in the now sealed silence that it painfully brings to us:

> *Speak, you too,*
> *speak the last to speak,*
> *say your saying.*

> *Speak—*
> *But do not separate the No from the Yes.*
> *Give your speech meaning too:*
> *giving it shadow.*

> *Give it enough shadow,*
> *give it as much shadow*
> *as around you you know is spread between*
> *Midnight Midday Midnight.*

Blicke umher:
sieh, wie's lebendig wird rings—
Beim Tode! Lebendig!
Wahr spricht, wer Schatten spricht.

Nun aber schrumpft der Ort, wo du stehst:
Wohin jetzt, Schattenentblösster, wohin?
Steige. Taste empor.
Dünner wirst du, unkenntlicher, feiner!
Feiner: ein Faden,
an dem er herabwill, der Stern:
um unten zu schwimmen, unten,
wo er sich schimmern sieht: in der Dünung
wandernder Worte.

["Sprich auch du," from *Von Schwelle zu Schwelle* (1955)]

Look all around:
see how that becomes alive all around—
In death! Alive!
Speaks true, who speaks of shadow.

See how the place where you are is contracted:
Where do you want to go now, you without
  shadow, where?
Climb. Feeling your way, climb.
Thinner, harder to recognize, finer!
That is what you are becoming, finer: a thread,
along which it wants to descend, the star:
to swim down below, all the way down below,
there where it sees itself
twinkling: in the swelling movement
of words that are always going.

to Henri Michaux
who, invisible, holds out his hand
to lead us toward another invisibility.

Leave.
Somehow leave.

The long knife of the stream of water
  will stop speech.

Michel Foucault
as I Imagine Him

A few personal notes. I have dwelled with Michel Foucault without any personal relationship. I never met him, except once in the courtyard of the Sorbonne during the events of May '68, perhaps in June or July (but I am told he wasn't there), where I spoke a few words to him, who was unaware of who it was speaking to him (whatever the detractors of that May might say, it was a fine moment, when everyone could talk to everyone else, anonymous, impersonal, a person among the people, welcomed without any other justification than being another person). It is true that, during these extraordinary events, I often said: But why isn't Foucault here?—thus restoring to him his power of attraction, and reflecting upon the empty place he ought to have occupied. To which people responded with a remark that did not satisfy me: he is still a little reserved; or: he is abroad. But actually a lot of foreigners, even the distant Japanese, were there. That is perhaps how we missed each other.

His first book, as it happens, which brought him renown, had been sent to me when that text was still just an almost nameless manuscript. It was Roger Caillois who had it and showed it to many of us. I recall Caillois's role, because it seems to have remained unacknowledged. Caillois himself was not always

I am not accepted by the official specialists. He was interested in too many things. Conservative, innovative, always a little apart, he did not enter the company of those who are the custodians of accepted knowledge. Last of all, he had forged a very beautiful style for himself, used sometimes to excess, until he began to think he was fated to keep watch—indefatigable watchman—over the proprieties of the French language. Foucault's style, in its splendor and precision—seemingly contradictory qualities—left him perplexed. He couldn't decide whether this grand baroque style didn't ruin the singular knowledge whose multiple characteristics—philosophical, sociological, historical—overwhelmed and excited him. Perhaps he saw in Foucault another himself, who hid his legacy from him. No one likes to recognize himself, a stranger, in a mirror where he discerns not his double, but the one he would have liked to be.

Foucault's first book (let's agree that it was the first) focused on relationships with literature that will have to be corrected later on. The word "madness" was a source of ambiguities. Foucault treated madness only indirectly, but above all focused on this power of exclusion that, any fair or foul day, could be implemented by a simple administrative decree, a decision that, by dividing society not into good and evil, but into reasonable and unreasonable, allowed us to recognize the impurities of reason and the ambiguous relationships that power—here, a sovereign power—would maintain with whatever there is that is most divided, while still letting it be understood that it would not be so easy for it to reign without dividing. The important thing is in fact this division; the important thing is exclusion itself—not what it is that one excludes or divides. Finally, what a strange thing history is, if a simple decree can overturn it, without great battles or important monarchic disputes. This dividing, which is in no way an act of mean-spiritedness, intended to punish dangerous beings because they have been determined to be asocial (idle, poor, debauched, foul-mouthed, extravagant, their heads empty or mad)—this dividing, then, through an ambiguity even more formidable, has to attend to the excluded by giving them medical care, food, blessing. To prevent the sick from dying in the street, the poor from becoming criminals just to survive, the debauched from perverting the pious by flaunting bad habits and giving them a taste for them, all that is not detestable, but marks some progress, the point of departure for a change that educators will deem excellent.

So from his first book forward, Foucault deals with problems that have always belonged to philosophy (reason, unreason), but he deals with them by the roundabout means of history and sociology, while privileging in history a certain discontinuity (one little event changes a lot), without making this discontinuity into a rupture (before madmen, there were lepers, and it is in the places—places both material and spiritual—left empty by the vanished lepers that the shelters for other excluded beings are established, just as this necessity to exclude perseveres under surprising forms that sometimes show it and sometimes hide it).

A Man in Danger

One has to wonder why the word "madness" (*folie*), even in Foucault, has kept a considerable power of interrogation. At least twice, Foucault will reproach himself for letting himself be seduced by the idea that there is a profundity to madness, that this madness might constitute a fundamental experience situated outside of history, of which poets (artists) have been and can still continue to be witnesses, victims, or heroes. If this was a mistake, it was beneficial to him, insofar as, through it (and through Nietzsche), he became aware of his lack of taste for the notion of profundity, just as he will track down, in discourse, the hidden meanings, the fascinating secrets, in other words the double and triple sources of meaning, of which one cannot come to the end except by disqualifying meaning itself as well as, in words, the signified and even the signifier.

Here, I will say that Foucault who, one day, defiantly proclaimed he was a "happy optimist," was a man in danger, who, without making a display of it, had a keen sense of the perils to which we are exposed, trying to find out which are the most threatening and which can be forestalled. Hence the importance the notion of strategy had for him, and thus he came to toy with the thought that, if chance had thus decided, he could have become a statesman (a political adviser), as well as a writer—a word he always objected to with varying degrees of vehemence and sincerity—or a pure philosopher, or an unskilled laborer, hence an anything or an anybody.

In any case, a man on the move, solitary, secret, who, because of that, is suspicious of the lures of interiority, rejects the traps of subjectivity, searching for where and how a surface discourse might be possible, one that mirrors, but without mirages, not foreign, as we thought, to the search for truth, but letting there be glimpsed (after many others) the perils of this search, as well as its ambiguous relationships with the various mechanisms of power.

Farewell to Structuralism

There are at least two books, one seemingly esoteric, the other brilliant, simple, engaging, both apparently programmatic, that seem to open the future to a new knowledge, and that are actually like testaments where promises are inscribed that will not be fulfilled, not out of negligence or inability, but because there might be no other fulfillment than their very promise, and by formulating them, Foucault reaches the end of the interest he brings to them—that is how in general he settles his scores, then turns to other horizons, without however betraying his demands, but masking them beneath a seeming disdain. Foucault, who writes prolifically, is all the more so a silent being: determined on keeping silence when well-intentioned or ill-intentioned questioners ask him to explain himself (there are exceptions, though).

The Archaeology of Knowledge, as well as *The Discourse on Language* [*L'ordre du discours*], mark the period—the end of the period—when Foucault, as the writer that he was, tried to expose discursive practices that are almost pure, in the sense that they refer only to themselves, to the rules of their formation, to their point of attachment, although without origin, to their emergence, although without author, to decipherments that would reveal nothing concealed. Witnesses who do not confess, because they have nothing to say other than what has been said. Writings that rebel against all commentary (ah, the horror Foucault had of commentary!). Autonomous domains, but ones that are neither truly independent, nor immutable, since they are continually being transformed, like atoms that are at once singular and multiple, if we are willing to grant that there exist multiplicities that do not refer to any unity.

But, you will say, Foucault, in this adventure where linguistics plays its role, does nothing else, with the intentions unique to him, but pursue hopes for an almost defunct structuralism. One would have to try to determine (but I am poorly placed for such an enquiry, for I note that up until now I have never uttered, either approvingly or disapprovingly, the name of this ephemeral discipline, despite the friendship I bore for some of its upholders) why Foucault, always so superior to his passions, becomes truly angry when people try to make him board this boat that already has such illustrious captains. The reasons are many. The simplest (if one can call it so), is that he still senses in structuralism a whiff of transcendentalism, for what about those *formal* laws that regulate all of science, while still remaining foreign to the vicissitudes of history on which their appearance and disappearance nonetheless depend? A very impure mixture of historical a priori with formal a priori. Let us recall the vengeful passage in the *Archaeology of Knowledge*; it's worth the trouble.

> Nothing, then, would be more pleasant, but more inexact, than to conceive of this historical a priori, as a formal a priori that would be, moreover, endowed with a history: great motionless empty figure that would rise up from time one day, that would create a tyranny to rule over human thought that no one could escape and then would disappear suddenly in an eclipse to which no event would

have given a foretaste: transcendental syncope, flickering play of forms. The formal a priori and the historical a priori are neither on the same level nor of the same nature: if they meet, it is because they occupy two different dimensions.[1]

And let us also recall the final dialogue of the same book where the two Michels are facing each other in a duel to the death where no one knows who will receive the mortal blow: "All throughout the book," says one, "you have tried, as best you could, to stand apart from 'structuralism' . . ." The reply of the other is important: "I did not deny history (while structuralism seems to have the essential characteristic of ignoring it); I held in *suspense* the general and empty category of change to make transformations of different levels appear; I reject a uniform model of temporalization."[2]

Why such a bitter, and possibly pointless, dispute (at least for those who don't see what's at stake)? Because the archivist that Foucault wants to be and the structuralist he does not want to be both consent (temporarily) to appear to be working only for language (or discourse) alone, from which philosophers, linguists, anthropologists, and literary critics all claim to draw formal (hence ahistorical) laws, while still letting it incarnate a pernicious transcendentalism that Heidegger will remind us of in two oversimple phrases: language does not have to be founded, since it is the one that founds.

The Demand
for Discontinuity

Yet, when Foucault concerns himself with discourse, he does not reject history, but distinguishes discontinuities in it, discretions, not universal ones, but local, that do not assume that from below a grand silent narrative perseveres, a continuous rumor, immense and limitless, which would have to be suppressed (or repressed), like a mysterious unspoken thing, or unthought, that would not only await its revenge, but would obscurely work in thought by making it eternally suspect. In other words, Foucault, who was never really taken by psychoanalysis, is even less ready to take into account a great collective unconscious, bedrock for all discourse and all history, a kind of "prediscursive providence" whose sovereign agencies—perhaps creative, perhaps destructive—we would have only to transform into personal significations.

The fact remains that Foucault, trying to distance interpretation ("the hidden meaning"), originality (a unique beginning brought to light, the Heideggerian *Ursprung*), and finally what he himself calls "the sovereignty of the signifier" (the imperialism of the phoneme, sound, tone, even rhythm), still continues to work on discourse to isolate within it a form to which he will give the unpretentious name of *utterance* [*énoncé*]: a word about which it must be said that it will be much easier to designate what it excludes than what it asserts (enounces) in its semiheroic tautology. Read and reread *The Archaeology of Knowledge* (a title that is dangerous in itself since it evokes what you must turn away from, the logos of the *archê* or speech of origin), and you will be surprised to find in it many phrases of negative theology, with Foucault putting all his talent into describing in sublime phrases what he rejects: "it is not . . . , nor is it . . . , but it also not . . . ," so that there remains almost nothing left for him to say to highlight the value of just what it is that is challenging the idea of "value": the utterance that is rare, singular, that asks only to be described or just reinscribed, in relation to just its *external* conditions of possibility (outside, exteriority) and thus giving rise to aleatory series that from time to time turn into an *event*.

How far we are from the profusion of phrases of ordinary discourse, phrases that keep generating themselves by an accumulation that contradiction does not stop, but on the contrary provokes to the point of a vertiginous beyond. Naturally, the enigmatic utterance, in that rarity that comes in part from the fact that it can be nothing but positive, without a cogito to which it would refer, without a unique author who would authenticate it, free from any context that would help to situate it in a conjuncture (whence it would draw its single or various meanings) is already by itself multiple or, more precisely, a nonunitary multiplicity: it is serial, for the series is its mode of grouping, having as its essence or property the ability to repeat itself (that is to say, according to Sartre, the relationship that is most stripped of signification), all the while constituting, with other series, an entanglement or a reversal of singularities that sometimes, when they come to a halt, form a *tableau,* or sometimes, by their successive relationships of simultaneity, are inscribed in fragments at once aleatory and necessary, comparable, it would seem, to the perverse (said Thomas Mann) attempts of serial music.

In *The Order of Discourse*, his inaugural lecture at the Collège de France (where, in principle, one says what one will do in the ensuing lectures, but that one will avoid doing since it has just been said and because this utterance can't bear being developed), Foucault enumerates, more clearly and perhaps less strictly (we might have to try and discover if this loss of rigor is due just to the demands of a lecture discourse or rather to the beginnings of a lack of interest in archaeology itself), the notions that must serve a new analysis. Thus, his suggestions *event, series, regularity*, and *condition of possibility*—he will use these terms to contrast word by word with the principles that according to him have dominated the traditional history of ideas; so he contrasts event with creation, series with unity, regularity with originality, and condition of possibility with signification, with the buried treasure of hidden significations. That is all very clear. But, from then on, doesn't Foucault provide himself with outdated adversaries? And aren't his own principles more complex than what his official discourse, with its striking phrases, would have us think? For instance, we take it for granted that Foucault, following a certain concept of literary production, rids himself purely and simply of the notion of subject: no more work, no more author, no more creative unity. But it is not all that simple. The subject

112

does not disappear: it is its unity, overdetermined, that is called into question, since what arouses interest and research is its disappearance (that is to say this new way of being that is disappearance) or even its dispersion that does not annihilate it, but offers us only a plurality of positions and a discontinuity of functions (here we find the *system of discontinuities* that, rightly or wrongly, seemed for some time unique to serial music).

Knowledge, Power, Truth?

Similarly, when Foucault is credited with a seminihilistic mistrust of what he calls a will to truth [*volonté de vérité*] (or thirst for serious knowledge) or even the suspicious rejection of the idea of reason (as having a universal value), I think we miss the complexity of his concern. Will to truth, certainly, but what is its price? What are its masks? What political programs are hidden beneath this eminently honorable research? And these questions are imposed all the more when Foucault, less out of a diabolical instinct than out of the destiny of modern times (which is also his own destiny), feels himself condemned to being attentive only to questionable sciences, sciences he does not like, suspicious already by virtue of their extravagant appellation of "human sciences" (it is the human sciences he is thinking of when he announces, with a kind of cheerful spite, the imminent or probable disappearance of man, who preoccupies us so, whereas we are doing everything to make him, starting today, posthumous, by our curiosity that reduces him to being nothing but a simple *object* of investigation, statistics, even surveys). Truth costs us dearly. We do not need to remember Nietzsche to be certain of this. Thus in *The Archaeology of Knowledge*, where we seem to delight in the illusion of the autonomy of discourse (an illusion with which literature and art might be enchanted), the multiple relationships of knowledge and power are announced, and the obligation to make us aware of the political effects that are produced at certain moments in history by this ancient desire to sort the true from the false. Knowledge, power, truth? Reason, exclusion, repression? You must be unfamiliar indeed with Foucault if you think he is content with such simple concepts or such facile links. If we say that truth is itself a power, we won't be much further along, since power is a useful term for polemics, but almost unusable as long as analysis has not withdrawn from it its catchall quality. As to reason, it does not have to give way to unreason. What threatens us, as well as what serves us, is less reason than the various forms of rationality, an accelerated accumulation of rational systems, a logical vertigo of rationalizations that are at work and in use in the penal system as well as in the hospital system, even the school system. And Foucault gives us this oracular sentence to inscribe in our memory: "The rationality of the abominable is a fact of contemporary history. The irrational, however, does not acquire its inalienable rights."

From Subjection to Subject

The book *Discipline and Punish*, as we know, marks the passage from the study of discursive practices alone to the study of the social practices that comprise its conditions. It is the emergence of politics in the work and life of Foucault. In a certain way, the preoccupations remain the same. From the great confinement [*renfermement*] to the various forms of impossible prison, there is just one step and in any case no "leap" [*saltus*]. But the chain of events (an appropriate term here) is not the same. Confinement is the archaeological principle of medical science (and Foucault will never lose sight of this imperfect knowledge that obsesses him, that he will find even in the Greeks, and that will end up avenging itself on him by abandoning him, powerless, to his fate). The penal system, which goes from the secret of torture and the spectacle of executions to the refined use of "model prisons" where one can acquire university degrees, while others have recourse to the satisfied life of tranquillizers, refers us to the ambiguous demands and perverse constraints of a progressivism that is nonetheless unavoidable and even beneficial. Any person who learns about where he comes from can marvel at being what he is, or, remembering the distortions he has undergone, can give in to a disillusionment that will immobilize him, unless, like Nietzsche, he has recourse to genealogical humor or to the lightheartedness of critical games.

How did people learn to fight the plague? Not just through isolating plague victims, but by the strict grid layout of the afflicted space, by invention of a technology of order from which later on the administration of cities will benefit; and finally by minute investigations that, once the plague has disappeared, will serve to prevent vagrancy (the right of "people of limited means" to come and go), to the point of forbidding the right to disappear, a right that is still refused to us today under one form or another. If the plague of Thebes has its origin in Oedipus's incest, one can deduce that genealogically the glory that is psychoanalysis is only a distant result of the ravaging plague. Hence the famous statement attributed to Freud [who said to Jung: "Don't they know we're bringing them the plague?"], when he arrives in America, but about which one can wonder if he meant by it that plague and psychoanalysis were originally and nosologically linked and, hence, were symbolically interchangeable. In any case, Foucault was tempted to go further. He recognizes, or thinks he recognizes, the origin of "structuralism" in the necessity, when the plague spreads, of mapping space (both physical and intellectual) in order to determine, according to the rules of a strict survey, the sinister regions of the illness—an obligation to which human bodies, both in the military arena and later on in schools or hospitals, learn to submit, and to become docile, and function as interchangeable units: "In discipline, the elements are interchangeable, since everyone defines himself by the place he occupies in the series, and by the distance that separates him from the others."

The rigorous gridwork that forces the body to let itself be searched, disarticulated, and, if necessary, reshaped will find its completion in Bentham's utopia, the model Panopticon, which demonstrates the absolute power of total visibility. (That is precisely the same as Orwell's fiction.) Such a visibility (the one to which Hugo exposes Cain even in the tomb) has the tragic advantage of rendering useless the physical violence to which the body would otherwise submit. But there is more. Surveillance—the fact of being under surveillance, which is not just what is exercised by vigilant guards, but which is identified with the human condition when one intends to make it at once responsive (conforming to the rules) and productive (hence useful)—will give rise to all the forms of observation, investigation, and experimentation without which there would be no real science. And no power either? That is less certain, for sovereignty has obscure origins that are to be sought on the side of expenditure rather than use, not to mention even more harmful organizing principles when they perpetuate the symbolism of blood, to which today's racism continues to appeal.

That duly noted and indicated, one has the feeling that, in a certain way, Foucault would almost prefer the openly barbaric times when tortures hid none of their atrocity, when crimes, having infringed upon the integrity of the Sovereign, established singular relationships between High and Low, so that the criminal, while he spectacularly paid the penalty for breaking the rules, preserved the glamour of the deeds that set him apart from humanity. (Thus Gilles de Rais; thus the accused in Kafka's *The Trial*.) The proof is that executions will not just be the occasion for celebrations at which the entire population rejoices, since they symbolize the suppression of laws and customs (we are in the realm of the exception), but sometimes provoke the people to revolt, that is to say, give them the idea that they, too, have the right, through rebelling, to break the constraints imposed on them by a temporarily diminished king. Thus it is not out of benevolence that the fate of the condemned is made more discreet, any more than it is out of kindness that the bodies of the guilty are left intact, to tackle their "souls and minds" instead, so as to correct or rectify them. Of course, not everything that improves prison conditions is detestable, but improvements do risk deceiving us about the reasons that made these ameliorations desirable or fortunate. The eighteenth century seems to give us a taste for new freedoms—and that is very good. Still, the foundation of these freedoms, their "substrate" (says Foucault), does not change, since we still locate it in a disciplinary society whose powers of mastery are hidden even as they multiply.[3] We are always increasingly more subjugated. From this *subjection*, which is no longer so crude but has become subtle, we draw the glorious consequence of being *subjects*, free subjects, capable of transforming into science the most diverse methods of a lying power, insofar as we have to forget its transcendence by substituting for the law of divine origin the various regulations and reasonable procedures that, when we are weary of them, seem to us to have emerged from a bureaucracy, human indeed, but monstrous (let's not forget that Kafka, who seems to describe brilliantly the cruelest forms of bureaucracy, also bows down before it, seeing in it the strangeness of a mystical, scarcely degenerated power).

The Innermost Conviction

If we want to see how much our legal system depends on an archaic substratum, it is enough to remember the role that the almost incomprehensible notion of "innermost conviction" plays in it. Our interiority not only remains sacred, but continues to make us the descendants of the Savoyard Vicar. And the analytics of moral conscience (*das Gewissen*) in Heidegger also draws support from this aristocratic heritage: inside us, there is a speech that becomes sentence, verdict, absolute assertion. This first utterance, removed from all dialogue, is the word of the law, which no one has a right to dispute.

What should we conclude from this? As to prison, Foucault comes to assert that it is of recent origin (but the dungeon wasn't invented yesterday). Or—and this matters more to him—he notes that prison reform is as old as the institution itself. Which, in one corner of his mind, signifies the impossible necessity to reform what is incapable of being reformed. And then (I will add) doesn't monastic organization demonstrate the excellence of isolation, the wonder of being face to face with yourself (or with God), the superior benefit that comes from silence, a propitious place where the greatest saints are formed and the most hardened criminals created? Objection: the former consent, the latter are forced. But is the difference so great, and aren't there even more rules in convents than in jail cells? Finally, aren't prisoners serving a life sentence the ones who have sworn *perpetual* vows? Heaven, hell, the distance is either minute, or infinite. What is at least certain is that, just as Foucault does not call into question reason in itself, but rather the danger of certain rationalities or rationalizations, so also he is not interested in the concept of power in general, but in the relationships of power, in their formation, their specificity, the way they are put in play. When there is violence, everything is clear, but when there is compliance, it might only be the result of an inner violence that is hidden in the heart of the most assured consent. (Foucault has been reproached for neglecting, in his analyses of power, the importance of a central, fundamental power! Whence people deduce what they call his "apolitical" stance, his rejection of a struggle that might one day be decisive—the final conflict—and his lack of any plan for universal reform. But people pass over in silence not just his immediate struggles, but his decision not to play with those "great projects" that might be no more than useful alibis of daily servitude.)

Who Is Me Today?

In my opinion, Foucault's difficult, but also privileged, position can be considered this way: do we know where he stands, since he does not see himself (in a perpetual "slalom" between traditional philosophy and abandoning any spirit of seriousness) as a sociologist, or as a historian, or as a structuralist, or as a thinker or metaphysician? When he performs detailed analyses that relate to medical science, to the modern penal system, to the extremely varied uses of micropowers, to the disciplinary subjection of bodies, or finally to the immense domain extending from the confessions of the guilty to hearing the confessions of the righteous or to the endless monologues of psychoanalysis, we wonder if he is just sampling certain facts that have value as *paradigms*, or if he is retracing historical continuities whence the various forms of human knowledge appear, or finally if he is strolling (as some accuse him) haphazardly, through the field of known or preferably unknown events, in fact cleverly choosing them to remind us that all objective knowledge remains dubious, just as the pretensions of subjectivity are illusory. Didn't Foucault himself confide to Lucette Finas: "I have never written anything but fiction, and I am perfectly aware of this"? In other words, I am a fabulist composing fables, the morals of which it would be imprudent to anticipate. But Foucault would not be Foucault if he didn't correct or qualify himself right away: "But I think it is possible to make fiction function within truth." Thus the idea of truth is certainly not dismissed, any more than is lost from view the idea of subject, or the inquiry into the constitution of man as subject. I am sure that the remarkable book by Claude Morali, *Qui est moi aujourd'hui?* [*Who Is Me Today?*] would not have left Foucault indifferent.[4]

Who shall I wear today?

Society of Blood, Society of Knowledge

Yet Foucault's return to certain traditional questions (even if his answers remain genealogical) was precipitated by circumstances I won't claim to elucidate, since they seem to me to be of a private nature, and it would serve no purpose to know them. He explained himself, without being entirely convincing, about the long silence that followed the first volume of his *History of Sexuality*, *The Will to Know*, which is perhaps one of his most attractive works in its brilliance, its incisive style, its assertions that overturn commonly held notions. The book is directly descended from *Discipline and Punish*. Never has Foucault so clearly explained Power, which is not exercised starting from a single, sovereign Place, but comes from beneath, from the depths of the social body, deriving from local, mobile, transitory, sometimes minute forces, to the point of developing into powerful homogeneities whose convergences make them hegemonic. But why this return to a meditation on power, while his current reflections now center on revealing the mechanisms of sexuality? For a number of reasons, only two of which I will focus on, a little arbitrarily: because by confirming his analyses of power, Foucault means to challenge the claims of the *Law* that, while keeping watch over, even forbidding, certain sexual manifestations, continues to assert itself as essentially constitutive of Desire. And, too, it is because sexuality, as he understands it, or at least the punctilious importance we grant it today (a today that goes a long way back), marks the passage from a society of blood, or one characterized by the symbolism of blood, to a society of knowledge, norms, and discipline. Society of blood: that means glorification of war, sovereignty of death, justification of torture, and finally the grandeur and honor of crime. Power speaks, then, essentially through blood—whence the value of lineages (having a noble, pure blood, being unafraid of shedding it, and at the same time a prohibition of dangerous mixtures of blood, whence the modifications of incest laws or even an appeal to incest precisely because of its horror and prohibition). But when power renounces its links with the privileges of blood and sanguinity alone (under the influence also of the Church, which will draw profit from it by overturning the rules of marriage—for instance, suppression of the levirate), "sexuality" will take on a preponderance that will associate it no longer with the Law, but with the norm, no longer with the rights of masters, but with the future of the species—life—under the guidance of a science that tries to determine everything and regulate everything.

The passage, then, is from "sanguinity" to "sexuality." Sade is the ambiguous witness to it, and its fabulous demonstrator. Only pleasure matters to him; only the order of *jouissance* and the limitless right of sensual pleasure count. Sex is the only Good, and the Good rejects any regulation, any norm, except (and this is important) the one that invigorates pleasure through the satisfaction of violating it, even if this be at the cost of the death of others, like death exalting itself— supremely happy death, without remorse and without anxiety. Foucault says then that "Blood has resorbed sex." This conclusion surprises me, though, since Sade, that aristocrat who, even more in his work than in his life, takes the aristocratic into account only to take pleasure in flouting it, establishes the sovereignty of sex to an unsurpassable degree. If, in his dreams or his fantasies, he likes to kill and to accumulate victims in order to push the boundaries that society, or even nature, might impose on his desires, if he likes blood (less than sperm, though, or, as he says, "fucking"), he is not in the least concerned about maintaining a pureblood caste, or one of superior blood. Quite the contrary: the Society of the Friends of Crime is not held together by aspiration to some ridiculous eugenics; transgressing official laws, and bonding by secret rules, that is the cold passion that gives sex and not blood its primacy. A morality that revokes, or thinks it revokes, the fantasies of the past. So that we are tempted to say that, with Sade, sex seizes power, which naturally signifies also that henceforth power and political power will be insidiously wielded by using the mechanisms of sexuality.

Deadly Racism

It was as he was pondering the transition of a society of blood to a society where sex imposes its law and where law uses sex to impose itself that Foucault saw himself, once again, confronted with what is still, in our memory, the greatest catastrophe and the greatest horror of modern times. "Nazism," he says, "was the most naïve, thus the most cunning, combination of blood fantasies and disciplinary paroxysms." Blood, indeed: superiority through exaltation of blood pure of any kind of mixture (a biological fantasy that conceals the right to mastery accorded to a hypothetical Indo-European society, the highest manifestation of which would be Germanic society), the obligation, henceforth, to preserve this pure society by suppressing all the rest of humanity and, first of all, the indestructible heritage of the people of the Bible. The implementation of genocide needs power in all its forms, including the new forms of a bio-power whose strategies impose an ideal of regularity, method, cold determination. Men are weak. They accomplish the worst only by ignoring it until they are accustomed to it and find themselves justified by the "grandeur" of a rigorous discipline and the orders of an unquestioned leader. But, in the history of Hitler's rule, sexual extravagances played a minor, quickly suppressed role. Homosexuality, the expression of wartime comradeship, just provided Hitler with a pretext to destroy the unsubdued groups, which were nonetheless in his service, but which, undisciplined, still found traces of the bourgeois ideal in ascetic obedience, even if this was obedience to a regime that asserted itself as above any law, because it was law itself.

Foucault thinks that in order to prevent the proliferation of mechanisms of power that deadly racism was about to abuse monstrously (by controlling everything, including everyday sexuality), Freud sensed the need to go back, which led him (by the sure instinct that made him the privileged adversary of fascism) to restore the ancient law of marriage, that of "prohibited consanguinity, of the Father-Sovereign": in a word, he restored to the "Law" its previous rights to the detriment of the norm, without however sacralizing prohibition, that is, the function of repression, the mechanisms and origins of which (censure, regression, superego, etc.) it then became important for him to expose. From this arises the ambiguous nature of psychoanalysis: on one hand, it lets us discover or rediscover the importance of sexuality and its "anomalies"; on the other hand, it summons around Desire—in order to ground it, even more than to explain it—all the ancient order of marriage; thus it does not take the side of modernity, and even constitutes a sort of formidable anachronism—what Foucault calls a *"historic retroversion,"* a designation whose danger he will see, since it seems to imply he is favorable to a historical progressivism and even to a historicism from which he is actually quite remote.

The Determination to
Talk about Sex

It should perhaps be said at this point that, in his work *The History of Sexuality*, Foucault does not take lightly the fight he wages against psychoanalysis. But he does not hide his penchant for seeing in it only the completion of a process closely linked with Christian history. Confession, avowal, examinations of conscience, meditations on the straying of the flesh—all place the importance of sexuality at the center of existence and finally develop the strangest attempt at a sexuality that is diffused throughout the entire human body. What people try to discourage is encouraged. What until now had remained silent is given speech. What people would like to repress is given a unique value, thus making it obsessional. From the confessional to the couch, there is the journey of centuries (for a lot of time is needed to accomplish a

139

few steps), but, from sins to delights, then from secret murmuring to endless chatter, we find the same determination to talk about sex, at once to free oneself from it and to perpetuate it, as if the only occupation, in the aim of making oneself master of its most precious truth, consisted in consulting oneself and consulting others on the cursed and blessed domain of sexuality alone. I marked a few sentences where Foucault expresses his truth and his humor: "We are, after all, the only civilization where workers are paid for listening to people confide about their sex . . . they have put up their ears for rent." And this ironic judgment on the considerable time spent and perhaps lost putting sex into words, into discourse: "Perhaps one day people will be surprised. They will be hard put to understand how a civilization so devoted to developing immense systems for production and destruction had found the time and the infinite patience to wonder with so much anxiety about sex; they will perhaps smile, remembering that these people we were believed there is in this matter a truth at least as precious as the one we had already asked of the earth, the stars, and the pure forms of thought; they will be surprised at the single-minded determination we put into pretending to snatch from its night a sexuality that everything—our discourse, our customs, our institutions, our regulations, our knowledge—produced in full daylight, and revived with uproar . . ." Little fragment of a reversed panegyric where it appears as if Foucault, from this first book in *The History of Sexuality*, wants to put an end to those vain preoccupations, to which nonetheless he plans to devote a substantial number of books—which in the end he did not write.

Oh My Friends

He will look for and find a way out (it was in brief a way to remain a genealogist, if not an archaeologist) by distancing himself from modern times and questioning Antiquity (especially Greek antiquity—the temptation we all have to find our "sources" there; why not Judaic antiquity, where sexuality plays a large role, and where the Law had its origin?). To what end? Apparently to go from the torments of sexuality to the simplicity of pleasures, and to illumine with a new light the problems they still pose, although they occupy the attention of free men much less, and escape the joy and scandal of the forbidden. But I cannot keep from thinking that, with *The Will to Truth* [*La Volonté de savoir*], the vehement criticisms this book aroused, the kind of mind-hunt (like a "manhunt") that followed from it, and perhaps too some personal experience I can only guess at and that I think he himself was struck by in ignorance of what it represented (a sturdy body that ceases to be so, a serious illness he had hardly any presentiment of, finally the approach of a death that opened him not to anguish, but to a surprising and newfound serenity)— all those profoundly modified his relationship to time and to writing. The books he went on to write on subjects that still intimately involved him, are, at first sight, books of a studious historian rather than works of personal research. Even their style is different: calm, tranquil, without the passion that makes so many of his other texts scorching. Interviewed by Hubert Dreyfus and Paul Rabinow[5] and questioned about his projects, he suddenly exclaims, "Oh, first I'm going to attend to myself!" A statement that is not easy to shed light on, even if one thinks a little hastily that, following Nietzsche, he was inclined to look toward the Greeks less for a civic morality than for an individual code of ethics that would allow him to make his existence—whatever existence was left for him to live—into a work of art. Thus he will be tempted to ask the Ancients for the revaluation of the arts of friendship, which, without ever being lost, have not since been highly valued, except by a few of us. The *philia* that, for the Greeks and even for the Romans, remains the model for whatever is excellent in human relations (with the enigmatic character given to it by its opposing requirements: at once pure reciprocity and generosity without return), that sense of friendship, can be welcomed as an inheritance always capable of being enriched. Friendship was perhaps promised to Foucault as a posthumous gift, beyond the passions, the intellectual problems, the dangers of life, which he felt for others more than for himself. By bearing witness to a work that needs to be studied (read without prejudice) rather than praised, I think I remain faithful, even if clumsily, to the intellectual friendship that his death, which was for me so very painful, permits me today to declare to him, while I remember the phrase attributed by Diogenes Laertius to Aristotle: "*Oh my friends, there is no friend.*"

Notes to *Michel Foucault As I Imagine Him*

1. All translations from *The Archaeology of Knowledge* are my own. For reference, see Michel Foucault, *The Archaeology of Knowledge*, trans. A. M. Sheridan Smith, New York: Pantheon, 1972, p. 128. —Trans.

2. Translations are my own. For reference, see *The Archaeology of Knowledge*, pp. 199–200. —Trans.

3. "The Enlightenment, which invented freedoms, also invented discipline." (That is perhaps an exaggeration: disciplines date back to prehistoric times, when, for instance, through successful training, they turned the bear into what would later on be the guard dog or the valiant policeman.)

4. Claude Morali, *Qui est moi aujourd'hui?*, preface by Emmanuel Levinas, Paris: Editions Fayard, 1984.

5. Michel Foucault, *Un parcours philosophique*, Paris: Gallimard, 1989, a study to which I am greatly indebted.

who shall I wear today·

Today goes a long way back

from secret mummeries to endless chatter

as a child painstakingly made-up a language to allow her difference was all to be different

146